Cinco de Mayo

Julie Murray

Abdo Kids Junior
is an Imprint of Abdo Kids
abdobooks.com

Abdo
HOLIDAYS
Kids

abdobooks.com

Published by Abdo Kids, a division of ABDO, P.O. Box 398166, Minneapolis, Minnesota 55439.
Copyright © 2019 by Abdo Consulting Group, Inc. International copyrights reserved in all countries.
No part of this book may be reproduced in any form without written permission from the publisher.
Abdo Kids Junior™ is a trademark and logo of Abdo Kids.

Printed in the United States of America, North Mankato, Minnesota.

102018
012019

 THIS BOOK CONTAINS
RECYCLED MATERIALS

Photo Credits: Alamy, AP Images, Getty Images, iStock, Shutterstock

Production Contributors: Teddy Borth, Jennie Forsberg, Grace Hansen

Design Contributors: Christina Doffing, Candice Keimig, Dorothy Toth

Library of Congress Control Number: 2018945943
Publisher's Cataloging-in-Publication Data

Names: Murray, Julie, author.
Title: Cinco de Mayo / by Julie Murray.
Description: Minneapolis, Minnesota : Abdo Kids, 2019 | Series: Holidays set 2 |
    Includes glossary, index and online resources (page 24).
Identifiers: ISBN 9781532181726 (lib. bdg.) | ISBN 9781532182709 (ebook) |
    ISBN 9781532183195 (Read-to-me ebook)
Subjects: LCSH: Cinco de Mayo (Mexican holiday)--Juvenile literature. |
    Holidays, festivals, & celebrations--Juvenile literature. | Fifth of May (Mexican holiday)
    --Juvenile literature. | Mexico--Social life and customs—Juvenile literature.
Classification: DDC 394.262--dc23

Table of Contents

Cinco de Mayo

Cinco de Mayo is a
Mexican holiday.

5

It is on the 5th of May.

7

It celebrates Mexico winning a big **battle**.

8

9

There is a **parade**.

Rosa dances.

Luis waves a Mexican flag.

It is green, white, and red.

A Mexican band plays.

People enjoy food.

Juan eats mole.

16

Lola hits a piñata.

The candy falls.

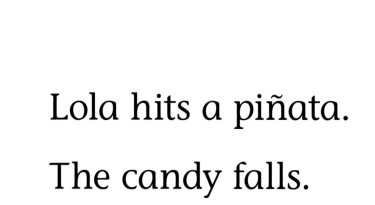

Maria loves Cinco de Mayo.

Signs of Cinco de Mayo

Mexican band

Mexican flag

parade

piñata

22

Glossary

battle
a fight between two armed forces during a war.

mole
a flavorful sauce that is often served on festive occasions.

parade
a public procession of people, music, and more in front of a crowd as part of a celebration.

Index

Abdo Kids ONLINE
FREE! ONLINE MULTIMEDIA RESOURCES

Visit **abdokids.com** and use this code to access crafts, games, videos, and more!

Abdo Kids Code:
HCK1726